SKETCHES AROUND THE FAL

Sue Lewington

Sue Lewington is a professional artist and lives on St. Martin's Isles of Scilly where she has her own gallery.

This is her third collection of sketches. Her previous books on St Ives and the Isles of Scilly are much enjoyed by her admirers.

Published by Dyllansow Truran, Croft Prince, Mount Hawke, Truro, Cornwall TR4 8EE.

Printed by R. Booth at the Troutbeck Press, Amron Hill, Mabe, Penryn Cornwall TR10 9HH.

ISBN 1 85022 129 4 (cased)
ISBN 1 85022 130 8 (paperback)

The river never seems
still. White sails &
brightly coloured
tripper boats are
always passing ~
then you turn a corner
& its all peace &
quiet & a small boat
sitting on its own
perfect reflection :

3

4

St Anthony lighthouse
a bright, blowy day - sailing boats everywhere;
the working boats racing in their Sunday best;?

Just some steps in the middle of a beach. The tide brings on the boat people get on and get off. And just the Ferry waiting for the boat its gone...

ST. MAWES TO PLACE FERRY

St. Mawes Castle

St Mawes from the sea. A Sunday afternoon's
sail from Malpas.

7

8

THE St MAWE HOTEL

St. Mawes
Exotic trees, tiny gardens,
bright greens — little lanes
leading steeply uphill &
glimpses of shining water
& distant trees through
narrow alleyways.

I wish I hadn't started this one. The perspective is awful...

9

St MAWES
TREGONY 10½
LONDON 263¼
SAFETY FIRST

Shell

ROSELAND GIG CLUB

2/3d gallon
Sorry Sold out!

SHELL

SHELL

PREMIUM

REGULAR

2/3d gallon
Sorry Sold out!

2/1d gallon
Sorry Sold out!

Mending nets on the quay
- a good job for a
quiet winters day

Dating from the 6th century the arch is 15th Century

ST. MAWES HOLY WELL

LETTER BOX

An old letter box set into the Auto-living wall at a house.

11

Huge ships like skyscrapers
in the middle of the river, such a strange sight

The TAMAMIMA of NASSAU & a
Russian ship - I forgot to get the
name.

12

St. JUST CHURCH AND BAR

13

falling tide, peaceful reflections

14

15

Cottages + boats at St. Clement

16

Decoration along an old shed by the road.

a cottage by the Church

Around St. Clement.

18

post box on the gate of a cottage

19

TRURO

The Cathedral towers
over the back streets
& the river.....

...ere is a little mission church built in ...e churchyard. Today it is decorated ...r Harvest Festival!

The stone pillar outside the door was found in the foundations of the old church & may be pre-christian...

...mpkins & cabbages, onions & apples, fruits & flowers

orange

...hite

yellow

...orange

only the tower remains shrouded in ivy, home to masses of rooks, hidden by trees, or are they crows?

21

22

COWLANDS
A lovely place to sit & stare – which is a good thing because the car won't start.

BOAT FOR SALE

RIVER'SIDE

APPLES EATERS COOKERS

cottage called RIVERSIDE which is practically in the river at Coombe.

23

OLD KEA CHURCH – just the top of the tower above the trees

TRELISSICK HOUSE – looking downriver to the sea it must have one of the best positions possible.

THE KING HARRY FERRY – looking quite different from the river – usually I'm sitting in the car onboard... It runs quietly back and forth all day saving miles of driving & giving a peaceful breather from the roads

KHF

TRELISSICK GARDEN

A view across some of the garden's beautiful
hydrangeas, looking upriver towards Tregothnan
House which along with Trelissick commands
the best views of the Fal. (well — I'd have built there too!...)
The hanging woods are sliced off a few feet above
the beach by the action of the salt water, r huge
rusting vessels find a temporary home in the
deep water channel. So incongruous here ...

25

PILL CREEK

A quiet day at Feock. No wind, tide dropping fast. Very still. My only company a spaniel chasing fish (I think) in the shallows & a squirrel chattering & complaining to himself & dropping acorns on me...

27

DEVORAN

cold afternoon, low tide, stones, mud & shining water. All around are the remains of the days when Devoran was a large, busy port — before the river silted up. Ruins of large stone sheds & mooring stones which are obviously suitable for large ships, not the small boats here today. The large stones on the quay are, I think, the remains of the old tramway which ran where the (narrow) road is now.

All so quiet now......

29

The Pandora - thought I'd have lunch & paint at the same time only to find the place hidden by a forest of scaffolding. Very interesting watching the thatchers at work though.

Under the scaffolding is a beauti rambling building full of uneven windows & doors & huge chimney

IN MEMORY OF THOMAS JAMES AGED 35 years

who on the evening of the 7th Dec.
1814 on his return to Flushing from
St. Mawes, in a boat, was shot by a
Custom house officer & expired in
a few hours after.

Officious zeal in luckless hour laid wait
And wilful sent the murderous ball of fate
James to his home (which late in health he left)
Wounded returns - of life is soon bereft

In
memory of mr
Joseph Crapp. ship
wright who died 26th of
Nov 1770 Aged 40 years
Alass Frend Joseph
His End was Allmost Sudden
As thou the mandate came
Exprefs from heaven
his foot it Slip And he did fall
help help he cries & that was all

MYLOR CHURCH

FLUSHING

Greenbank Falmouth

swans on the road, right
opposite 'swan cottage'
& a view across to
Falmouth

32

THIS WALL
ONCE FORMED A PART OF
THE
GREAT CELLARS
BUILT IN 1709 AS
STORAGE FOR
THE POST OFFICE
PACKET SERVICE
1689 – 1850

SWAN COTTAGE

Flushing is full of
quite different architecture.
Elegant houses with pillared & decorated doorways.
the Packet Captains had money to spend when they moved over
here from Falmouth.

33

Boats, sails & oars in a shed just above the Quay

34

FOR SALE
£500 OR
OFFERS
0116 70330

Low tide mud every shade of mauve, blue
& brown & silky pale shine

35

PENRYN

Rows of boats, old & very old..
being done up... & rotting
away. All of them beautiful...
I could spend days here painting,
walking & looking......

36

FY 10

37

Falmouth from Flushing

38

39

CUSTOM HOUSE QUAY   Falmouth

40

41

Not a car... but a boat parked by the back door!

42

wandering around with Mark on a snowy February day - down alleyways to the water & tiny landing steps & bits of quay, built on & hidden...

Everywhere you look
boats of all sizes,
vans loading, men
working & talking

43

44

Glimpses of Falmouth

Penrose
Sailmakers

FH546

45

The King's pipe

CUSTOM HOUSE QUAY
The first quays were
built here in 1670
full of small
fishing boats &
bustle . . . .

KING'S PIPE

FORMERLY USED FOR
THE DESTRUCTION OF
CONTRABAND TOBACCO

46

PENDENNIS CASTLE.
And coastguard Station

I know now where the coastguard & weather reports on the radio every morning come from..

mca A.M. COASTGUARD

The views from the road around the castle are wonderful - over the docks, across to St Anthony, up river & then round the coast to the Helford & beyond. But the castle itself can barely be seen. 47

PRINCE OF WALES PIER — ferries coming & going to St. Mawes, Flushing & on longer river trips

RIVER FAL   HELFORD RIVER   St. MAWES

FALMOUTH'S LARGEST
HELFORD RIVER BOAT
MV TUDOR PRINCE
sailing daily to view
FRENCHMAN'S CREEK
HOUSE OF MANDERLEY
From the Film
REBECCA

DEPT (WCP)   RET
11.00 a.m.   1.00 p.m.
2.30 p.m.   4.00 p.m.
The only Triple deck boat on the
HELFORD RIVER

HELFORD RIVER

TUDOR PRINCE
&
PRINCESSA
Nr S STEPS LEFT
SIDE OF PIER
YOU MAY PAY
ON BOARD

THE FLUSHING FERRY

48

ADRIAN GILBERT

ST. MAWES FERRY

ST. MAWES FERRY

Winter Timetable

Dep.t Falmouth	Dep.t St. Mawes
8.30 a.m.	9.00 a.m.
10.15 a.m.	10.45 a.m.
11.15 a.m.	11.45 a.m.
1.15 p.m.	1.45 p.m.
2.15 p.m.	2.45 p.m.
3.45 p.m.	4.15 p.m.

Please pay on board
W.m CP.